Orts and All

*More Ribald Rhymes
and Gay Doggery*

. . . .
I thought, if I could draw my paynes
Through rhime's vexatyon, I sho'ld them allay.
Grief brought to numbers cannot be so fierce,
For he tames yt that fetters it in vearse.

John Donne
(The Grosart Edition, 1873)

II

Orts and All

*More Ribald Rhymes
and Gay Doggery*

Clive Murphy

Brick Lane Books
London

Very best wishes & thanks for, friendship, & John & Ann

from

Clive

23/7/03

I found the gaffe (is the whole thing a gaffe?) on P. 16 yesterday, Nemis died.

Published in 2003 by Brick Lane Books
132 Brick Lane, London E1 6RU
Tel: +44 (020) 7247 6626
Web: website.lineone.net/~brick_lane_books

ISBN:
0-9541563-1-5

British Library in Publication Data
A CIP catalogue record for this book is available from The British Library

Cover illustration by Adam Graff

Printed by Publish on Demand Ltd.
22-24 Highbury Grove,
London N5 2EA

Headings set in Elevator
Text set in Sabon

Distributed by the Publishers

AT THE DOGS IN DULWICH
The Memoirs of a poet
PATRICIA DOUBELL

A STRANGER IN GLOUCESTER
The Memoirs of an Austrian in England
MRS FALGE-WAHL

A FUNNY OLD QUIST
The Memoirs of a gamekeeper
EVAN ROGERS

DODO
The Memoirs of a left-wing socialite
DODO LEES

ENDSLEIGH
The Memoirs of a river-keeper
HORACE ADAMS

In preparation:

APRIL FOOL
The Memoirs of a former prep school headmaster
EVAN HOPE-GILL

ANGEL OF THE SHADOWS
The Memoirs of a cat lady
JOAN LAUDER

OUTCAST
The Memoirs of a transvestite
DAVID A. SHERRIFF

For
I.G.

Apologia

Some writers fear to be a friend,
From amity are barred,
And, quite until their bitter end,
Behave uncommon hard.

But tolerate the lives they lead
And led and will lead later.
They dare not say it's you they need -
Their books may prove your traitor.

C.M.

Contents

Christmas Eve

I saw Daddy kissing Santa Claus
Underneath the mistletoe last night.
I questioned why. He said because
They'd drunk too much, were tight.
Sober, plastered, so bloody what?!
The pair of them are queers.
I've never heard such tommyrot -
They've snogged for years and years.
The next time, I'll expect a yacht,
A kite, a train, a drum,
A flashlight, mega-mega-watt,
Or else I'm telling Mum.

Chameleon

Plying his trade in Mincing Lane,

Up and down and back again,

His "pedal extremities feel the strain."

Working the East End's Cable Street,

His after-dark, down-market beat,

He's "killed" by "bleedin' plates of meat."

Candlestick

"Use less Silvo, Mr. Schmidt!
Rub, rub, rub's the trick of it."

The Ivy

Thesps eat oats
With fancy blokes.
They do it at The Ivy.
If I'd a quid
I would, too.
Wouldn't you?

On Being an Iron and a faggot

'Bad queer', 'good gay'...
Labels, labels all the way.

Glam Domesticity

A housewife, whose life was a fake,
Thought she looked like Veronica Lake.
When she told the au pair
To get lost in her hair,
She obliged, calling, "Silence! First take!"

Curt Refusal to Join Golf Club

"Not up to snuff -
Too little rough."

Polite Reply to Country Invitation

"Regrets. I decline, though I pine by the hour.
I'm allergic to rape and, I'm told, it's in flower.

The English When Strangers Address Them

Don't speak,
Don't smile.
Think, "Bloody cheek!"
And run a mile.

What have All American Waiters in Common?

Pushing basket.
Need one ask it?

Two Reasons for Keeping My Socks On

"Why do you wear your socks in bed?"

"Because I've got cold feet," I said.

"I'll turn the heating up some more."

(He failed to 'get' the metaphor.)

To tell the truth, I'd an added worry:

My feet weren't washed - came out in a hurry.

"Please may I take your photograph?"

(14.5.03 after Readings at the Queen Elizabeth Hall to celebrate the 50th birthday of the Arts Council of England's Poetry Library)

Carol Ann Duffy

Did not rebuff me.

Urinal

In the next stall a cyclist stands
Chortling to himself, "No hands!"

Can't Aim in
Pub Loo

So this is the meaning of 'blind drunk':
The floor in water deep is sunk;
The place is for ducks you would have thunk.

Little Poet

Pasty
But tasty.

Prude

A pile of pants
Without the ants

Frustrated Voyeur

The saddest man I ever met
Bought twenty beefers as a set.
He keeps them in a big glass box
To watch them getting off their rocks
And hasn't seen one do it yet.

Butcher in Shorts

No underwear consolidation -
What a dangly sprawl!
The belief his meat's a treat for all
Is quite without foundation.

Teacher

Mr. Chips
In nipple clips.

To a Castrated Shepherd

"You've cheated me, as sure as hell.
In future wear a wether-bell!"

fetish

Archie thrilled to pants and knickers
Worn by leapers, spinners, kickers.
Ballet, tap, Greek, anything -
A glimpse would stir his ting-a-ling.
For stalls, Row A, he paid a packet -
Near the band, despite the racket.
Men's or Ladies' didn't matter,
Though, if pushed, he'd choose the latter.
And, so long as convex crutch,
A private world beyond his touch,
Twinkled a second on the stage,
Its owner could be any age.
Blood into his cheeks would rush
In an anticipatory flush
While the overtures resounded
Before at last the artistes bounded,
Kaleidoscopes of vim and thrust,
Augmenting his peculiar lust.

Mistress Paige, she was sublime;
Cilla as Jack in pantomime;
Not to mention Whirly MacLaine
Or, freed from Madam[1], Hey-there! Wayne[2]...

[1]Dame Ninette de Valois [2]Wayne Sleep

15

These were stars but 'gypsies' backing them
Fully pleasured Archie, lacking them:
A batch of Redcoats (ex-Pwllheli)
Could do the work of a Minelli.
Lavish productions at the Prince Edward
Ravished his id, rendered him leadhard.
Numbers provided the best confection.
Numbers offered most to lech on.

Archie spent thousands, saved not a penny,
On substitute sex - the real stuff not any.
Hard to explain in a month of Sundays
How dear is a liking for Showbiz undies.
And when, at eighty, a job even small
Was refused - "Too old, mate!" - he owned
fuck all,
Unless you count a meagre Pension,
Income Support and a travel subvention.
So how was found some meat and drink
For his raison d'être, his little kink,
Increased not diminished by social privation,
Without its turning to brute fixation
And making an oddball having fun
whom C.M. Into a fiend from who you run?
The answer is simple and somehow right:
By loss of marbles, a gentle flight

From threatened poison, brain-stagnation,
To safe, creative liberation.

I saw him only yesterday.
His Final Curtain's near, I'd say,
But he's content. To a satiety
Life offers colour-packed variety,
As round about the streets he'll wander
Washing-lines to ogle, ponder
Whenever airstreams gust and flow,
In other words, laundry's on show,
Placed outside in proliferation
For wind to cause evaporation.
On lawns beyond back-garden gates,
On balconies of grim estates,
Row upon row of clothes and sheeting
Have dotted there, his senses heating,
Smalls embodied in his fancy
By ev'ry Ginger, Fred and Nancy
Performing, just for him especially,
A show that suits him to a T,
Where all are naked to the knee,
Mouvementés, flashing treats for free.
See him joyous at their flapping,
Side by side and overlapping!
Happy punter, he'll die clapping.
God bless Archie! R.I.P.!

Two Kentish Apples. October, 2001

Red-hard and juicy, fallen from grace,
They lay in the grass at Penshurst Place.

The Apple of My Eye

Love is a many-splendoured thing -
or so proclaims the song.
Yet why, when making love to you,
Do I feel I'm doing wrong?
I'll answer my own question:
It's your looks that I adore;
I know beneath that patina
You're rotten at the core.

'What Isn't Sex' (field Report)

Tarrant Hinton[1]
Agrees with Clinton[2]
Exhausted.

Winton[3]

[1] A Dorset village
[2] A former President of the United States
[3] Not the TV celebrity, Dale Winton

Epitaph for a Wrestler

Won triple gold.
Lost moral hold.
End of life:
Floored by wife.

Epitaph for Peter Rabbit

In adulthood was claimed by vice.
Never left the same hole twice.

A Mother Talks of the Deprivations of Public School

"Tarquin's sex life is too narrow:

Of fun he gets no crumb

Except when playing against Harrow

Who grope him in the scrum."

An American Fisherman's Tale

"This dude, he had a latern jaw,
Dimpled deep as sin.
My rod's the longest in Arkansas
And it fitted in his chin."

Easing the Pain

Why do I drink gin and Scotch by the vat?
Because you tell lies at the drop of a hat.

He's Really Quite Nice Underneath

A sheep in wolf's clothing.
Full of self-loathing.

Epitaph for an Adolescent Boy

Sought friendship in the lonely city.

Be moved to pity.

Cynical British Tourist Rejects Offer of Long-term Relationship

"You only want a visa.

Think I'm not streetwise?

There ain't no flies on me, sir.

I avoid domestic Thais."

Hardcore Christianity

Bent?

Repent

Straight?

God's mate.

Chaff,

Wheat;

Naff,

Elite.

Church Exchange

"Penny for your thoughts."

"Bedroom sports."

"Whom with?"

"Joseph and Sydney,

Not Bessie, Smith."

Scottish Nightmare

An urchin cursed me in the ling.
I feigned I had a tawse.
He cried, "To use on me that thing
Is dead against our laws!"
I said, "My son,
Will you use one
On me? I hear they sting."

I stood there like a silly sheep,
Meek as a bellwether,
Held out my hand
But, I'll be damned,
He scarpered, hell for leather.

And now I find I cannot sleep,
Can't piece my soul together,
Because I frightened that wee creep
In the bonnie Highland heather.

Essex Man

Sports a jerkin.
Hides a merkin.

Two Points of View

Beaten in youth, he's now a beater,

Tabbed by shrinks as a 'repeater'.

I find this line a poor excuse -

The best react against abuse.

We have free will upon this earth:

The man is lacking moral worth.

Overheard Lapses of Political Correctitude

"Women, we know, are always shrewish.

Israelis, too, can't help being Jewish.

But a spazzy, helmeted, buttfucked runt

Needn't behave like a pain in the cunt."

The Agency Sent a Negro

All night to me the blues he sang.
I'd be happy with his whang.

Off-putting Doorstep Announcement

He gave me a last lingering kiss -
A blessing to unite us?
I wish he hadn't then said this:
"I think I've gingivitis."

Jenny Mackilligin

Though very, very fond of Adam*
I doubt in fact you ever had him.

*Adam Johnson, the homosexual poet, who
died tragically of AIDS in May, 1993

Scarlet Silk Instead of Newspapers

Lines his drawers -
Male menopause.

Rich Old Whore

Rouged, pneumatic cockatrice;
Expert, earning his weight in ice.

Crime Passionel

There once was a farmer called Ned
Who fell for a Rhode Island Red.
His wife wasn't daft:
"In the henhouse," she laughed,
I'll expect you to make your own bed."

But that wife of the farmer called Ned
Who fell for the Rhode Island Red,
When she found it was male
Took the axe from its nail.
Now Ned isn't living: he's dead.

Lunch Hour Assignation with PA

"How time flies! I've got to run.
Make a note I owe you one."

E-mail

Sorry,Rube.
Out of lube.
Fit u in
Tomorrow. Wyn.

What's Sauce for the Goose Should Be Sauce for the Gander

She makes me furious -

Far too curious.

I'd like to ask *her* a thing or two

But, needless to say, that 'wouldn't do'.

Hardened Explorers

Two homophobes, while in the Arctic,
Huddled for warmth. Results? Cathartic.

Clone

What lets you fuck it, then gets scary
When you call it Nellie or Mary?
The oxymoron of the prairie:
Corn -haired Jack, the Canada Fairy.

Churchill to Novello

"One mistake
Does not a bugger make."

Growing Old with Sister

I played with dolls. She called me 'sissy'.

I play with men. She takes the pissy.

I'm glad I've always been myself.

Now, like my dolls, she's on the shelf.

Fare Enough

A Paddy by the name of Stan
Is an open tart. We call him Flann.

Awkward Irishman at Naturist Colony

"What's your name?"

"Me name is Pat."

"Do you like this?"

"No, I like dat."

"Do you like these?"

"No, I like dose."

"Where are you going?"

"To put on me close."

Materialistic Neighbour

I've drilled through the wall to assess Mr. Quirke.
He's a sod with the spunk of an Istanbul Turk.

Though the same can't be said for his pal, Mr. Fitch,
I'd rather be him - he's infertile but rich.

Alzheimer's

Exhausted due to over-use of member.
With whom, when, and how, he never can
remember.

Post-Gig Heroin

"Me Tarzan.
He Jane."
Ape-rape. Insane.

Morning. Five-star hotel.
Pop star swings from vine
Amid penthouse hell.

Saturday Night on The Isis

Up for grabs

Catching crabs

Unavailing Protest by a Member of the force

A TV chef, not talking proper,

Was stuffed by a well-spoken copper.

"I trust that this truncheon

Enhances your luncheon."

"Not arf! Oi loves munchin' a whopper!"

Hurt

I know a man in Hackney.
He always wears a hood
(I'm told it hides bad acne).
With harness it looks good.

I asked him, in a back room,
"Does your face get smelly?"
He took me by the scrotum
And knocked me into jelly.

Two Tumblers

Praise heaven above!

A twist and a shove

And they're head over heels in love!

Shakespeare's to Blame

I wish he'd written 'glitters' -
It was 'glisters' I've been told.
I'd like this ending better:
'All that clitoris is not gold."